The Essential Hits of
Shorty Bon Bon

Also by Willie Perdomo

Smoking Lovely

Where a Nickel Costs a Dime

The Essential HITS *of* SHORTY BON BON

Willie Perdomo

PENGUIN POETS

PENGUIN BOOKS

Published by the Penguin Group
Penguin Group (USA) LLC
375 Hudson Street
New York, New York 10014

USA | Canada | UK | Ireland | Australia | New Zealand | India | South Africa | China
penguin.com
A Penguin Random House Company
First published in Penguin Books 2014

LIBRARY OF CONGRESS CATALOGING-IN-PUBLICATION DATA
Perdomo, Willie.
[Poems. Selections]
The essential hits of Shorty Bon Bon / Willie Perdomo.
pages cm.—(Penguin Poets)
Includes bibliographical references.
ISBN 978-0-14-312523-5
I. Title.
PS3566.E691216A6 2014
811'.54—dc23
2013043007

PRINTED IN THE UNITED STATES OF AMERICA

3 5 7 9 10 8 6 4 2

Set in Chaparral Pro with Brush Script

Designed by Patrice Sheridan

for Pedro Perdomo

Contents

Preface

In the mid-1970s, m   Pedro Perdomo (or "Cortijito," as
he was known in Sp.   larlem music circles) played per-
cussion on live studi   lings of Charlie Palmieri's classic
albums *The Cesta All   , Vol. 1* (1975) and *The Cesta All-
Stars Salsa Festival, Vo.   .976). The Cesta aesthetic could be
summed up in one word. *descarga*. I have never seen my uncle
play, nor did we ever meet. The following *descarga* is for his
memory on the night of his death.

Listen. That first of all.

—MARCOS RODRÍGUEZ FRESE

LIKE BREAD

What we remember to leave
Behind & forget: the dead
Survived in whisper, names
Added to a list. So many
Stones shaped into stories,
Hearts broken over bread.
To find word for what is lost
Requires falling, a brilliant
Wondering where next to tell
Our tales, what accounts can
We place in the ledger when
All we have left are the pieces.

W. E. P.

How I Came to My Name

"*Once that red light flicks on there's no time to fix mistakes, Poet.*"

HOW I CAME TO MY NAME

Palmieri points his first finger
Straight at my heart & says,
You—Shorty bon bon blen
Blen bip bap—don't squeeze
Too hard, this ain't rehearsal.
Don't go promoting half-truth
—Reap assassin-like. Pretend
Your neck is cuffed & booked;
Sold, then shipped. Play lyric,
Not ink. Do thread, not pocket.
Go reel-to-reel double-muscle:
Cuero y alma. Don't ask for a
Thing, don't flinch—stop only
In heart-stops & when you feel
Like it's on the money—jump.

BEMBÉ-FACED

Trombones discharged their fat mugs.
Sat on a few bars before the pocket
Players drew their best shot. Then I
Shook all the safety from their style.
Came in mega-dirty, dressed to seek.
Big-thumb, bully-bass & blossoms—
Bro, my soul had spotlight to spare.
How to play it again? In back-to-back
Hurricane time, a spirit snapped from
Spool, bembé-faced in chocolate snow.
Yes, Poet—swear to life—like I said:
That night, I put the dong in the ding.
In shadow-speak, light was my king.

THE BIRTH OF SHORTY BON BON (TAKE #1)

If you want to argue
why, why we keep pointing
to salsa for glue, for true
federation, check out the
kingdom hall of dance, everyone
yelling yes yes yes, no one
shooting back. When a pair
of eyes meet on a bandstand,
all the dreamers start talking
in history tones: fated,
trimmed, breaking
night into revelation, ready
to globalize social clubs.
How did Shorty play it again?
Like his birth certificate
was lost forever.
Best to leave impurities to
diamonds, forget the way
batteries go dead, bury all
the masters until a later date—
too late to use your fingers, just
listen, listen to the coro, they'll
let you know
when the page is blank
between you and your grave.

ARROZ CON *SON Y CLAVE*

My father used to leave sharp sounds
By the door, steady conga heads were
Rare. When you party with grown-ups,
You learn not to suffer dancers a weak
Hand; otherwise a safe return to silence
Becomes less of a road—no yesterday.
The great readers, he would say, quote
From the kitchen. Yes, chops—cook,
Steam like jabs, stories, walls that sob
I'm sorry. In the middle of a sacrifice,
Death always has a shape to introduce:
Breath deflates & balloons a club like
An amateur soul drowning in whisper.

SANGRE VIVA

For the blood sounds, court war from heart.
Live by concrete & corner store, by coconut
Husk & empty can. Go get Tony Timbales,
Pablo el Negro, Ray Hard Hands, all of us
Who guttered fast, possessed to trade curses.
Bandstand-to-studio cats lived sand-quick &
Left spines to fry on fences—scared to jump.
(Our tombs blazed like blackout summers.)
When Our Thing went Tropical, styles hung
Soft, hardcore numbers couldn't bust grapes
In Napa. Manager-turn-promoter-turn-mogul
Dispatched spies to catch & copy our repeats—
Always, always carry at least one new roll &
Jet before a jukebox punks your last selection.

THE BIRTH OF SHORTY BON BON (TAKE #2)

Shorty Bon Bon knew
the Great Street
would ask for a cut.
He jammed out like ceremonies
were on curfew, like his
left hand was a nail,
his right hand a hammer.
The lifelines on his palms
began to split and look
for second takes.
Listen, he used to say.
The conguero who plays
like the club is on fire,
is always the first
to disappear in flame.

START FROM THE END GOING TOWARD THE END

What I remember between first & last track
Is how I replied to voice-sweet pretty boys.
About my schooling, my training, how to cop
These wicked skips, open slaps, double-time:
What could I say but point to my ears, Poet?
From hook-to-lug, stave-to-skin, rim-to-head,
The fires were sweet, the grooves waterproof.
I smoked bottom off barrel & brim off bucket.
The catalog I sampled tread a line of aunts &
Uncles—all dead to the bone. Never paid for
Class, never signed up for fancy, but I always,
I always listened when the gods came to sit in.

SYNCOPATED LICKS

Begin & end with a syncopated lick.
First with your right, then back again
With your left. To be real, I had masters
Back against the wall, thirsty for loops:
Cinder-blocked fingertips, piss-treated
Calluses, skin-loud & stacked with *son*.
The jump was so jumping that my red
Bandana pin-dropped & buckled like a
Leaf falling new, lobes tickling happy,
A crispy voice custom-made by storm.

I'm waxed down to a tight bounce.
    You laid me out in the sun to cure.
Open up. Make room for your devil.
    Go hard-hands. Dig fire out of me.

Man, I mean-galloped phrase-to-bar, flew
From zero-to-Mars in blasts & blips, Poet,
But never so high that I couldn't fall again.

THE BIRTH OF SHORTY BON BON (TAKE #3)

The salseros, the real-live soneros,
the palo-players that gang-busted
dancehalls with fish-crate yambú;
the tumberos who recorded the earth
in clay jugs, whose steel-beam shoulders
held up skies until shing-a-ling
floors were occupied by the perfect
fourth of democracy; the quintets
that crashed baptisms and plucked
concert hall from park bench and
band shell, who glittered airwaves
without commission, who changed
their names from Joe Loco to Joe
Panama, Joe Ponce to Joe Cuba, who
Castkill'd then Corso'd, who
vamped it up and whistled evil
out of garden—their Africando
was so hot, co-op boards had to
call the police—this take is for
the cocolos who carried a nation
on their crazy, on their cool:
What you can say about Shorty
Bon Bon is that he never never
crossed the clave. He knew
it was all dirt at the end.

So cool
> That I chased God like he was on the run.

So cool
> That my fingers were chopped off, paraded bloody
> Down the avenue & I still monkey-wrenched a black
> Note, duffel-bagged a *flamboyán,* Mozambique'd it
> Until roosters cried sunlight & eggs.

So cool
> That when Puente heard my speed, I made him bite his
> Tongue. I'm saying—I made the Mambo King bleed.

So cool
> That St. Paul's used to open after hours so I could
> Practice my undersong & un-pitch my city ears.

So cool
> That with closed palm, heel-to-toe, note on the beam,
> I cleared the brush & stars went mute without me.

THE BIRTH OF SHORTY BON BON (TAKE #4)

You want to know
how a god heavy
duty outta sight
goes brain-funky
and falls asleep
upright eyes open?
How a god rocks
stream-clear and counts
a whole band into a drum?
The more he tried to answer,
the higher his ruin
would reach for breath.
You could tell when
Shorty played memory:
No circle, no microphone.
Without turning his head,
he saw everything.

THE WAS OF THINGS

You can always start with the *was* of things.
At first, the sky begs for attitude, someone to
Thunder. For lack of reading skills, no boogie
To boast with, I took my time in old darkness,
Made center from flag & fracture. Come fist,
Came fight, I destroyed foe, fiend, all-star &
Saint—set-to-session, *timbales*-con-timpani.
Cast this lyric in fairy dust, bear its head just
Enough that it doesn't get bit & you would be
Putting a bomb where no threat is said to exist.

If you were to cut Shorty open,
out would spring Rose like a wind-gusted
boulevard, a rooftop
call for love and war, a late-night
radio dedication, a gat to your chin,
a boy with a flag, a dragon chase,
a notebook full of dreams and numbers,
a rock dove, slush, sleet, jelly
rolls, singers choking on charity,
a broken vase, one second, ribbons,
gifts, presents, riffs, showers, caked
blood, red table runners, plastic cups,
ice picks, emergency money, those choo
choo sounds from back in the day—
Truth told, Shorty played Rose like
she was a virgin with one ear.

To Be with You

"I asked Rose to sing and she told me not to follow the dead when they visit my dreams."

THE SOUL MAY BETTER UNDERSTAND

Rose's first note carried
Beautiful black faces,
Guts & apocalypses.

Badass blew the Sahara
Out of a dry run.

One night she invited Wrong & Right
Backstage to a fair one—
Beat the ditty out of both.

Truth, beauty? Day-long
Knuckle-for-knuckle duets.

Just imagine, Poet:
Your house is burning down
And there's no fire escape
To bust free of form.

DEAR SHORTY (NO. 1)

Listen to the key,
love me.
Pay for your
life up front,
let me eat
from every tree,
no judgment eyes.
Be crystal,
crash into me
like a new star,
like the ground
rips open just for us.
Act like you know
my name, whatever
you say has to eat
water and dance.
Be gentle when you
talk, pretend you got kicked
in the head by a mule
and when you lost vision,
the first thing you heard
was my song.

DELICIOUS NUMBERS

Islands of dancers repeated themselves. And me
With a living-room two-step & two-tone heel,
Tried my best to scat with each tip of my—shit,
Rose once crooned a badge off a detective's hem.

Trust me, Poet. I used to catch bandleaders drug
Revolutions & guzzle harmony into alleyways—
Rose could angel-trade songster for gangster.
(She dreamed numbers I couldn't divine.) It was
As if I got my first lesson in everything two/four,
Four/four, six/eight, half break & run, baby, run.

DEAR SHORTY (NO. 2)

Tell me, tell me, tell me how
we used to finish B-sides in the shower, how
your tongue was too tight for the truth.
Don't forget, I held your face like it was dust;
your eyes had nothing to claim.
It had to be the floor's stomp
wrapped around my ear meeting
in fair-fall. Tonight a share,
a share of stain is afraid
to touch the songs we flung
off bridges. If only
you could split a river
the way horizon opens sky,
as if to dive in and stretch.
Yes, my love, I know for sure
what's buried in my dirt:
The rain kisses, our last photo and
the way you walked past like before
you could mess with me, you had to
deal with your muertos.

THE CITY OF YOU

The scene was treated with a breakfast fix,
Even the priests stopped inventing for free.
Out came the mandolins for the mandarins,
Violins for the vespers—Our Thing, *mano*,
Was definitely for the stay-alive, the *sangre*
Viva, the sacred & snake, too. When Rose's
Throat hit six-figures, she bit razors in half,
Sucked on nightmares, Fame chipped a tooth.
Not one, bro, but six attempts to blank a page
Plus one pearl treasured in long grain, voyage
Bottom-booked. Told her twice in downbeat,
Told her once up-tempo: Babe, you can be the
Center of your song, but you can't be the star.

DEAR SHORTY (NO. 3)

What I believe myself to be
is never understood.
Before you said a word,
I saw you boost my love
letters from the rubble.
I saw you post up in halls
and lobbies, parks and
churches, start hobbies
you couldn't pay balances on.
I choose not to count all the places
where we found ourselves broken
for the calling we couldn't hear,
the heard that went undone.
Give me sun, give me moon, give me star—
miracles roll solo, no witnesses.
I still can't remember
who turned off the boogaloo
on our basement party.

HOW IT WENT DOWN

It went down like this, Poet:
The bolero to that morning's
Departure knew when to end.
It swept yesterday's mess
Off the front step, meditated
On the things we hang dry.
Rose and I used to fuck freshly
Squeezed, until our swear
Words went blind. Her love
Was super disco-fevered:
A community of vicious
Handclaps, a quick bump
In the ladies' room & the eyelids
On her charts would slam shut.

DEAR SHORTY (NO. 4)

And if you saw me
falling, what
would you yell
from the Great Street?
What is all this shit you talk about
when you talk about love?
This zoo-bang, this funhouse,
could be swing, could be
slide, this ball, this diesel,
what is this thing you call
cure and sickness?
Tell me, tell me, if you
feature or go first, what
good is reason to the last set?
When you read the stains
at the bottom of my coffee cup,
be careful, you might feel
more like a monster than a tree
and what looks like a monster
is really a tree.
If I had a license
you might say, True.
You might say
that all the beautiful
discoveries usually come
late to the party.

MAYBE UNDER SOME OTHER SKY

Ask me, Poet, *Did I love her?*
Breast against bristle, penny eyes—
I loved Rose the way fours
Exchange blows, the way fractures
Need islands, the way we tremble
In the glow of dead-ass truth—
You wanted to stay awake
Just to see the end with her.

Guardian, gladiator & goon—
Skeleton-to-ash—speak, dead.
Forget, always. Ask me again,
    Did I love her?
With holy-mouth & hard-hand,
I play like I say: Yes. Yes I did.

DEAR SHORTY (NO. 5)

Fuck with me
and I will give you
passage on layaway.
I will make you drop to your knees
in after-party silence until
your dreams are overcrowded.
I will be the mosquito in your
eye at last glance, make you
scream in your sleep
until the lyrics on my lips
turn to ice, until
your last whereabouts
are so unknown
that each fig
will be put to rest
and your heart
can't find a corner to stand on.

WHEN THE CURE IS WORSE THAN THE SICKNESS

C'mon, baby, Rose said.
I said, No. I'm staying right here.

Self-divided, she
Touched everything.

I want to show you something.
Show me from here.

Her pubis snaked into platinum clefs.
Ven, papito—

Squirted standing ovations—
Te quiero, mucho.

Toma, she said, the word *love*
Trickled from her lips.

Candlelit, she disappeared the way she appeared—
No encore, no applause.

DEAR SHORTY (NO. 6)

In my new healing, I learned
that we are all sick.
To start, you begin here
and end up
where you've always been.
The dream-cries stay
in the background, the crashing
sound of best against you.
What cleaner stage
to be invisible, to be chosen.
The charms and laws
change faster than curtains.
When you come, come dressed
in mid-promise.
Anything, anything but
the past, please, just a clean
scrape, no stones—
I hear you can find
mistakes in heaven.

BLUES FOR ROSE

You call for news.
The news is bad.

By bad
You don't mean good.

Rose is gone.
If this were a blues,

You would sing it again:
Rose is gone.

DEAR SHORTY (NO. 7)

It's been a minute since
I had a blessing.
All I ever wanted
was to be untied,
to find Spring without
love, to win the battle
of forgetting you.
When it came to building,
I didn't have the hands for it.

Fracture, Flow

"In the dream, I was in Puerto Rico. It was raining and headless worms inched along the dates on my headstone."

HAVE IT YOUR WAY: COMBO

1. Official Business

Blunt lit, gaze ahead, puff waves & wait.
El Morro—your castle. The weed so good
You swear that *La Niña* is on the horizon.
You say, *Fuck it. Last set, time to bug out.*
When Columbus steps ashore, you call him
Negrito, you say, *Take off the brim, lose the*
Doublet, get rid of the girdle—it's hot, bro.
And you being the Paseo Boricua that you
Are, the dirt-eating Ponceña that you are,
The Don Filiberto that you are, the che-che-
Colé that you are, the thirty seconds it takes
To steal a car that you are, the olive-skin
Buddhist pop star that you are, will pass
Columbus the blunt & tell him to take a hit
Before government is shut down for the day.

2. Feliz Navidad

At the most notorious intersection in
Santurce, Anacoana sits under a palm
Tree & picks sarcoma off her cheeks.
When she spots your taxicab, she dips
A sloppy open back to outside turn &
Breaks into a rumba of "Jingle Bells."
She presses a super-sized Burger King
Cup against your window. Her eyes are
Spook-hollow, her habit trimester-big;
Crocodile tears beg epidemic chip-ins.
The *turístico* eats a red light, silences
You back to Creation, and before you
Can leave him a tip, he opens a *décima*:

When For Sale stops lying to Paradise.
When Paradise says, Enough, no más—
Land goes free, blood black, and brother,
You just ain't ready for that kind of noise.

3. Sanjuanero Swag

You enter La Cantera—toast ready.
Your swag—shellacked.
First thing you do
Is look for something empty,
Anything you can *voz*.

A shark fevers the pool table—sells
Bundles, no bank shots. All the canaries
Buy you frosted Medallas.

Dashes of balm & sunset, the copper
Of cowbell, melt in the sawdust. Eleggua
Reigns in, *quilombo*-quiet, vessel in hand.

Of course you can ancient, when he asks. Then
You drop a fresh word for scream, short for holy.
Really, you tell him all night—again & again—
That you play for Freedom.

4. Son de Lolita

Your fingers tremble
On each rosary bead.

You are a bush
Of *siemprevivas.*

Just yesterday
You had coffee

With the Virgin &
Her new man.

You defended
The dirt you ate.

You wanted to be a nun
But a gun

Convinced you
Of its higher power.

5. Conjugation Games

Now remember: your conjugation game
Needs to be tight. It's true: Puerto Ricans
Love for free & *coquís* are almost extinct.
When the set opens remember how Albizu
Blasted yanqui go home with that *me cago*
En la madre que te parió, cabrón. Center
Stage & make ceiling retreat. Break history
In positive spin cycles, flip it so dictionaries
Can't catch up—whip out your chain gang
Hum, antifreeze epic over here & then over
There. Go with your nerves; each finger-snap
A world, each world a last set. Play ghosts
Their funny kind of music lost in translation.

6. Fracture, Flow

There's no use muffling flaw or fault line.
The island is split like even booty & there's
Definitely no faking jacks at ocean's end.

Kneel, swear, kiss-the-ground & hope-to-die.
But fuck around, drop a mask & lose track of
The *son*—you better keep your lies to yourself.

7. Plaza Las Delicias

If you had to smuggle a score out of Egypt,
The password would be *Ponce*—

Dead-dog ballads for roasted pigs, *guayabera*
Dialogues, the deceased on town display—

A grant of heaven by block party, grass
Dust—a silent, immaculate lion—

Sundown fountain spurts—a fire engine
Stuck in massacre red.

8. How to Bum-Rush an Island & Blow Up the Spot

Over there is the same as over here:
Send a few soldiers into the block,
Blow it up with a few bricks—blau.
Give the slick cats their kickbacks,
Gas a king up, bum-rush, clean-chop
Heads off & boom—bag up the gush.

9. Noches de Galería

First Tuesday skin-bleached
Morenas, metrosexual eyebrows
Threaded to filament, free
Bomba clinics, machetes
Made of wood, cobblestone
Gleam & *vejigante* tricks—
Like a breeze of first tries
You choose to confide in trees.

On the flight back home
You dream of Isla Madre:
She walks into the nearest
Precinct, strapped head-to-
Achilles in dynamite &
Demands that the San
Juan Ritz-Carlton casino
Return all her SSI checks.

SHORTY BON BON'S FREEDOM SONG

Big man big man come here big man
Got these lady liberties big man shhhh
They might be listening big man come
Here big man let me show you some
Freedom look look look turn her upside
Down and stars come out of her O big
Man two-for-five three-for-ten trying
To make an honest living my name is
_____ but my friends call me Shorty
I ain't selling drugs I'm selling freedom
O you funny big man yeah you right they
Could be the same thing happy new year
Man I know you made some resolutions—
Look at this one here, she's bilingual but
That's gonna cost you extra big man c'mon
Big man work with me the boys are doing
Parallels trying to riddle me silly like I got
The bomb diggity c'mon now help me out
Big man on the freedom you know how it is
Brother, come get some—on the freedom.

The Birth of
Shorty Bon Bon:
Solo

"They say each saint will have its day. I say,
Give that bone to another dog."

THE BIRTH OF SHORTY BON BON (TAKE #6)

Tellers always ask,
If that will be all.
Told always says,
I didn't hear you.
Hey, man, don't nobody
wanna read your dedication.
Can you feel me in the back?
By the bling & the blab?
Can you fade this, brother?
Everything is leaving now.
The plan for today is—
Are you two? Are you one?
Are you forever? How much
is that money in the window?
You are new today, son.
Feliz, feliz a tu muerte . . .

You switch to a velvet booth, a short-circuited
Tombstone solo wears a cosmopolitan smirk—

Who is that copping pleas talking about
They haven't played that tune in a while?

Today is heavy-footed, branch-dumb, old
Standards grill the last call & outside

The skylines, the skylines are consumed by
One. Two. One-two-three—

Time to dig historic in that section of the circle
Where high call answers question with song.

Yes, Poet, I heard you.

And then what happened to Shorty Bon Bon?
He gave his last breath to Viejo San Juan.
Is it true what they say about Shorty Bon Bon?
No bird sells his wings, no sonero his son.
O, read me those poems about Shorty Bon Bon!
He buried his drum in La Plaza Colón.
O, tell me what happened to Shorty Bon Bon!
He lost his junjún in Viejo San Juan.

You lived on dreams & pauses for a whole take.
Whenever prayer shocked your fate lines, Buddha

Sang for pennies & his song blubbered the heavens,
The heavens went quiet with his laugh. The rocks

In your path were unemployed & there was enough
Space for a second life—sounds like just as it is—

Only way out was to be about something.

You—fly-guy with the hard hands, blade-swimmer,
Don't know if you heard but this horse is ready.
Gather your clouds & pearls, here comes lightning.
Put on grease & butter, eagle-colt, glass slipper,
Bitch mink, evil-faced guitar wail, O bongo, O
Agogo, kundalini & caduceus—clack-clack, oye
Como va, check my bon bon something nasty.

It is true—since birth your ears have been close
To the curb—for every initiation, a costly exit.

Recall the way bodies rocked, heads nodded,
Summers were fertile for fib stacked upon fib.

A platoon of funerals & shipwrecks marched
To pure end, wreaking spleen-to-spine havoc.

Still, you scraped dead skin off your fingertips—
All those hot beats & not one to go home with.

You—tar on the fence & mesmerized sin, sneak
Attack & crossfire—O, no, Voice, you dead flower
—before you go, grab my cowbell, my clave can
Divide by three & conquer-by-twilight—O clave,
Go, combust bleachers, warrior-call—thug-trychel,
Hang from my neck & party all night long.

A stone's skip away from my last
Wish to die clean, no stains left.
The heroic jam has been my life-
Long business, my ark of bones
Lay square inside the one & two—
Burning stairs call, time to go y'all,
The Great Street is now playing me.

Prince of catch-me-if-you-can,
Still trying to outrun the moon.
To hear you tell it, come the Great Street,
He'll have to scrape you off the corner
With the rest of the outlaws.

I tricked out bombs & slung bricks—
No mirror to be found. The angels
Rocked inferno stances, greedy
Chased greedy, night was dressed
In flight & snow told more tales
Than a dead man in a new world.

To hear you tell it, when He comes
Wolf-packing around the corner,
Jesus Christ can be on backup,
But He better know going in
That even Jesus Christ
Can get his jaw broken.

The price for my sonata non grata was
All good. Timber-yoked in mudslides—

Toca toca toca toca
Toma toma toma toma

The Great Street offered to buy me.
No exchanges, He said.

Vaya vaya vaya vaya
Juega juega juega juega

Didn't drop the secret then, no use
    Dropping it now.

The real never matches the display
Even when you try it one dream at a time—
Not looking kills you just as looking might.

Last chance to rewind, to pick up more
Than what's left & what you find funny
Is that nothing's funny—between future
And fury, what pulls you is here to stay.

"Rose—butter knife—that's your microphone.
Tony—fork & frying pan—you're on cowbell.
Pablo—dry red beans in the baby bottle—maracas.
Flaco—the pencils in the kitchen drawer—clave.
Me—I'll gig the empty garbage can. And Ray—
Bang on the wall until the horses come."

The bulb in my bicephalous heart
Dimmed down on Rose's soft glare—

No words, no air.

THE BIRTH OF SHORTY BON BON (FINAL TAKE)

Drum	*the ground in the zero*
Drum	*the quake in the earth*
Drum	*the one in the two*
Drum	*the death in the birth*
Drum	*the ran in the kan kan*
Drum	*the bomb in the bomba*
Drum	*the cha in the cha cha*
Drum	*the rumba rumbiao*
Drum	*the tumba tumbao*
Drum	*the dong in the ding*
Drum	*the pop in the smooth*
Drum	*the cry in the croon*
Drum	*the black in the hole*
Drum	*the sand in the time*
Drum	*the bend in the pitch*
Drum	*the reason the rhyme*
Drum	*the sugar the trade*
Drum	*the slap in the silly*
Drum	*the song in the belly*
Drum	*the moose in the call*
Drum	*glissando*
Drum	*glissando*
Drum	*you*

Notes

The Cesta All-Stars (originally known as the Alegre All-Stars) was founded in 1960 by Al Santiago, a Nuyorican (a Puerto Rican from New York City) bandleader. The word *descargar* literally means "to unload" but musically a *descarga* is a jam session. Inspired by the Cuban *descarga*, Santiago's arrangements included more vocal jocularity and improvisation, and because the Cesta All-Stars were a collective of some of that era's most formidable bandleaders and sidemen, the instrumentation was often phenomenal.

The verse by Marcos Rodríguez Frese is from his poem "Vital Poetics" ("Listen. That first of all. Then / unleash your tongue, your fists, / if necessary"), which appears in *Puerto Rican Poetry*, edited and translated by Roberto Márquez. Rodríguez Frese was a founding member of the *Revista Guajana*, a literary journal published at the University of Puerto Rico, Rio Piedras, in the 1960s.

"Like Bread": This poem was created as a component of a literary project at Yeshiva University Museum, New York, 2011. The poem was based on the museum's exhibition *There Is a Mirror in My Heart*, an installation by Sebastian Mendes. The poem's title is taken from Pablo Neruda's famous quote: "Poetry is like bread."

HOW I CAME TO MY NAME

"Shorty Bon Bon" (pronounced *bón bón*) literally means "short" and "sweet." In his introduction to *Aloud: Voices from the Nuyorican Poets Cafe*, Miguel Algarín, who founded the Nuyorican Poets Cafe, recounts a story of a homeless poet named Shorty Bón Bón, who walked into the café on a rainy night and recited a toast that became a "Loisaida classic," thus baptizing the opening of the café. He is a true urban legend. While this book is not informed by his legend, I use the name "Shorty Bon Bon" to honor and invoke our shared Nuyorican tradition and lineage.

"Bembé-Faced": "Bembé" is a Yoruban word. Its Afro-Cuban definition involves a ceremonial calling of a spirit. In Salsa NYC, if you were walking in El Barrio and asked someone, "Where's the *bembé*?" you would be asking, "Where's the jam, where's the music, where's the party?"

"Arroz con *Son y Clave*": The "*son*" was an outlaw genre and, according to Grammy-nominated musician and composer Bobby Sanabria, "the foundation of what today is called salsa." Its verbal improvisations, usually aimed at denigration (a dis, gossip, coded language, infidelities), were considered immoral but eventually became a tool for social protest and grew to cosmopolitan popularity. In Mary Kent's book, *Salsa Talks*, Israel "Cachao" López, referring to the *son* in Cuba during the 1920s, says, "The people who played the *son* were not socially accepted. Nobody wanted to own up to the *son*. The blacks accepted the *son*. Neither the middle class people, much less the people from the upper classes, wanted anything to do with the *son*." A *sonero*'s skill has always been a point of honor. "Clave" is the heart of Afro-Cuban-based music. In a note via e-mail, Sanabria explained the clave this way: "It is split up in either a 3 + 2 or 2 + 3 cadence depending on the rhythmic direction of the melody. Although tapped out by two sticks in traditional *son* music and rumba (of which the *son* and rumba have slightly different clave patterns respectively) it is inherently present in the music even if no one is playing the actual clave sticks."

"Sangre Viva": "Tropical" is a Latin music genre, preceded by *salsa romántica*. In interview after interview, the salsa musicians from the 1970s thought that the *salsa romántica* of the 1980s was the end of an era. Sanabria wrote, "The best way to describe it [*salsa romántica*] is as the de-Africanization of salsa," and the key was eliminating or minimizing the role of percussion and vocal improvisation. "Napa" refers to Napa Valley, a wine-growing region in northern California.

"Start from the End Going Toward the End": Title adapted

from an Ilse Aichinger quote. The quote appeared in an essay by Uljana Wolf titled "A Werldly Country: Ilse Aichinger's Prose Poems" (*The Poetry Project Newsletter*, February/March 2010, number 222). Referring to Aichinger's previous work, Wolf wrote, "In an earlier piece, Aichinger had proclaimed that the only possible way of narration that was left was 'from the end and towards the end'—the experience of fear, death, and nearly complete destruction became the starting point for a new narration, a new kind of writing."

"The Birth of Shorty Bon Bon (Take #3)": "Yambú" is an older, slower, Cuban rumba form. "Corso'd" refers to the Corso Ballroom, which fostered many of salsa's greatest artists. In *Salsa Talks*, many of the musicians also recall going to the Catskills to play at summer resorts. According to my father, *cocolo* is used to signify a die-hard *rumbero* or salsa lover. Thanks, Pop. Because when I first heard the word in 1970s East Harlem, it was the Puerto Rican version of the *n* word.

"How Cool Was I": "Mozambique'd" is a percussive style that, according to Sanabria, was created in 1962 by Mongo Santamaría's cousin, percussionist Pedro Izquierdo, a.k.a. "Pedro El Afrokan," in Cuba. "Puente" refers to Tito Puente, legendary bandleader.

TO BE WITH YOU

"The Soul May Better Understand": The title is taken from Dante Gabriel Rossetti's poem "Song and Music" ("Lean nearer, let the music pause: / The soul may better understand").

"Delicious Numbers": The title is taken from Robert Herrick's poem "To Music, to Becalm His Fever" ("Charm me asleep, and melt me so / With thy delicious numbers").

"The City of You": The title is taken from a verse in Mark Doty's poem "Almost Blue" ("This is the entrance / to the city of you"). The last couplet in "The City of You" was lifted from Anselm Berrigan. While a visiting author in Lewis Warsh's MFA class Writers on Writing at Long Island University/Brooklyn Campus, Berrigan answered a question about the use of first person in poetry, saying, "You can be the center of the poem, but you can't be the star."

"Maybe Under Some Other Sky": The title is taken from "Song That Can Only Be Sung Once" by Tom Sleigh ("Variable, changeable, yes, there are days when / people like us are like that. Maybe under // some other sky something like glory smiles on us").

"When the Cure Is Worse Than the Sickness": Riffs on the Tite Curet Alonso lyric *La cura resulta más mala que la enfermedad*" from "La Cura," a song he composed for Frankie Ruiz.

FRACTURE, FLOW

"1. Official Business": "El Morro" is a UNESCO World Heritage Site in Old San Juan. The Spaniards created this historic fort to ward off attacks on Puerto Rico. *"La Niña"* is the name of a ship in one of Christopher Columbus's New World fleets. *"Negrito"* is a shout to Pedro Pietri's verse ("Aqui to be called negrito / Means to be called LOVE") from his classic poem "Puerto Rican Obituary." "Paseo Boricua" is the legendary street in Humboldt Park, Chicago, that is bookended by two giant stencils of the Puerto Rican flag. "Filiberto" refers to Filiberto Ojeda Ríos, a prominent leader in the Puerto Rican independence movement. The FBI infamously gunned him down while serving an arrest warrant in September 2005.

"2. Feliz Navidad": "Anacaona" refers to the iconic Taino cacique. *"Turísticos"* are tourist taxis in San Juan. A *"décima"* is a poetic form popular in Puerto Rico. A particular trait of the *décima* is the introductory four-line stanza.

"3. Sanjuanero Swag": "La Cantera" is a neighborhood in Santurce, Puerto Rico. "Medalla" is a light beer manufactured in Mayagüez. "Eleggua" is a Yoruban deity, responsible for "opening the way." *"Quilombo"* refers to the Brazilian slave settlements.

"4. Son de Lolita": The title refers to Lolita Lebrón, Puerto Rican nationalist.

"5. Conjugation Games": "Albizu" refers to the leader and founder of the Puerto Rican Nationalist Party, Pedro Albizu Campos. *"Me cago en la madre que te parió, cabrón"* means, literally, "I shit on the mother who birthed you, motherfucker."
"7. Plaza Las Delicias": "Plaza Las Delicias" is the main plaza in the city of Ponce, Puerto Rico.
"9. Noches de Galería": The first Tuesday of every month used to be "Noches de Galería" in Old San Juan, a kind of street party when art galleries would stay open late into the night. *"Bomba"* is a folkloric Puerto Rican musical genre. *"Vejigante"*: demon masks made in Puerto Rico. "SSI checks": U.S. Social Security Supplemental Security Income, usually given to disabled adults and children and to folks who are over sixty-five who have limited means.

THE BIRTH OF SHORTY BON BON: SOLO

"Side A (3:2)": "La Plaza Colón" is a plaza at the entry into Old San Juan proper. "Junjún" is a two-headed African drum. "Agogo," from the Yoruban word for "bell," is an instrument used in Santeria rituals and more recently in samba.

Acknowledgments

Acknowledgments to the publications where earlier drafts of the following poems appeared:

> *Mandorla*: "Delicious Numbers," "The City of You," "Dear Shorty (No. 1)," and "Dear Shorty (No. 2)"
> *Mission at Tenth*: "How Cool Was I"
> *Huizache*: "Sangre Viva" and "Syncopated Licks"
> *Cura*: "Son de Lolita," "How It Went Down," and "Plaza Las Delicias"
> *H.O.W. Journal*: "Shorty Bon Bon's Freedom Song"
> *So Much Things to Say: 100 Poets from the First Ten Years of the Calabash International Literary Festival*: "Have It Your Way: Combo"
> Portions of "The Birth of Shorty Bon Bon: Solo" were published in *Union Station, Sun's Skeleton, 2 Bridges Review,* and *Tidal Basin Review.*
> *African Voices*: "Bembé-Faced"

Shout-outs and Big Ups

To repel ghosts you need a crew. I didn't write this book alone.
Shout-out to the following institutions:

Long Island University/Brooklyn Campus
Columbia University
Fordham University
Phillips Exeter Academy
Borough of Manhattan Community College
LEAP Program of St. Mary's College
University of Puerto Rico, Rio Piedras
Urban Word NYC
louderARTS Project
BookUpNYC, National Book Foundation
Lower Manhattan Cultural Council
New York Foundation for the Arts
Kingsbridge Heights Community Center
The Sonja Haynes Stone Center for Black Culture and
    History, UNC at Chapel Hill
VONA/Voices
Dark Room Collective
The Nuyorican Poets Cafe
Camaradas El Barrio
Harlem Arts Salon
El Museo del Barrio
La Casa Azul Bookstore
Tato Torres and Yerbabuena
The Crazy Bunch
Lounge 108
Caribe Social Athletic Club, Los Gallos
Capicú
HBO's *Def Poetry*
CantoMundo

Acentos
El Puente Academy
Cave Canem
La Respuesta, Santurce, Puerto Rico
PEN
CAMBA—
—Foundation and fellowship. Thank you.

Big up to Long Island University/Brooklyn Campus faculty and staff: Jessica Hagedorn, for finding the playwright in me, preserving the poet I used to be. Marilyn Boutwell—you cartographer you. Deborah Mutnick—for the narrative pull. John High—we're always crossing the river, brother. Jaime Manrique—for the personal essay. Vidhya Swaminathan—for research and methods. Michael Bennett—the seminar *is* the workshop. Harriet Malinowitz—teacher. Maria McGarrity—for Carib lit and blank pages. June Baird—for tsking tsking. Louis Parascandola—for Eulalie Spence and R train motivation. Patrina and Karen—for giving me yet another nickname. Lewis Warsh—in whose graduate Traditions and Lineages class Shorty Bon Bon was born on paper. Sealy Gilles—medievalist shepherd. Susan Halio—for the HEOP experience. Gladys Palma de Schrynemakers—for Smart Scholars.

Big up to Sarah Gambito—for my first university job. Heather Dubrow—for your advocacy and curatorial genius.

Shout-out to Linda Susan Jackson—this better get a Boogaloo pass.

Big up to Harold Augenbraum, Leslie Shipman, Rebecca Keith—you stand up for books, I stand up for you.

Shout-out to Lisette Norman, Eisa Ulen, Ms. Archipolo, Ms. Norman, Mr. Clarke, Sofia Quintero, Elisha Miranda—I would BookUp with y'all any day.

Big up to Michael Cirelli and the rest of the UDub crew—you kept sending me the new voices.

Big up to Roger Bonair-Agard, Marty McConnell, Lynn Procope, Guy LeCharles Gonzalez—for the Louder Arts in me.

Big up to Patricia Spears Jones—*femme du monde*.

Shout for Noel, for the *chez*.

Big up to Jon Sands—for that summer living room set

60

where I dropped some of these poems for the first time. Shout-out to Angel Nafis—for being front and center at the set.

Shout-out to Wesley Brown, Thomas Beller, Victor Lavalle, Noemi-Cress Martinez—for your push at Columbia. Gabriel Feldman, Zoe Townes—Morningside fam-a-lam.

Shout-out to Sule Greg Wilson. Your book *The Drummer's Path: Moving the Spirit with Ritual and Traditional Drumming* was a vital portal in this book's journey.

Big up to Bobby Sanabria—maestro. Your notes were masterful.

Shout-out to Mary Kent. Your oral history, *Salsa Talks: A Musical Heritage Uncovered*, gave me Joe Cuba's "crazy-bastard" recollections.

Shout-out to any and all existing members of the Fania All-Stars, the Alegre All-Stars, the Salsa All-Stars, the Cesta All-Stars. The rumba is still hot after all these years.

Shout-out to Jose Mangual, Jr.—for your real-on-the-money online interviews.

Shout-out to Emily Fragos and Kevin Young for your Everyman's Library anthologies: *Music's Spell* and *Jazz Poems*—respectively.

Big up to Paul Beatty, Dr. John Rodriguez (1974–2013), Maritza Stanchich, Odette Casamayor, Melanie Pérez Ortiz, Urayoan Noel, Patrick Rosal, and Carmen Muñoz Fernandez—your readings of earlier drafts helped the book jump.

Shout-out for Christie, for Windansea, for eternal sunshine.

Big up to Krista Franklin, Kevin Coval—Chicago jukes because of you.

Big up to Mayra Santos Febres and Guillermo Rebollo-Gil—for seeing the sound early.

Big up to my Long Island University/Brooklyn Campus MFA cohorts: Jani Perez, Liz Dalton, Patia Braithwaite, Lisa Rogal, Daniel Owen, Tony Iontosca, Michael Grove, Felice Belle, Uche Nduka, John Casquarelli, Aimee Herman, Guiseppe Infante, Micah Savaglio, Amyre Loomis, and Tiani Kennedy.

Big up to my students at LIU/Brooklyn Campus, Fordham University, BMCC, and St. Mary's LEAP—you were my soundboards and blank pages.

Shout for Julissa—the true heart's rumba.

Big up to my students at Phillips Exeter Academy—for the Harkness in you.

Shout-out to my Camaradaskies: Orlando Plaza, Rafael "Papo" Zapata, Ralphie Cruz, Merino "Rafa" Cortes, Tato Torres, Angelo Lozada, Isabel Martinez, May-Lin, Flaco Navaja—brokies, thanks for the brotivity.

Big up to Adrian Arrancibia, Stephanie De La Torre, and Reyes Rodriguez—West Coast connection. O.G.

Big up to Page meets Stage for setting up a reading with Afaa Michael Weaver—Mentor and Sensei.

Shout for Fabiola—for the mishu chants.

Big up to Paul Slovak at Penguin Books—dream-keeper redux.

Big up to Maria Massie at Lippincott Massie McQuilkin—thank you.

Big up to Jennifer C.—for the sessions.

Shout for Erika—for PLB *por vida*.

Shout-out to the Vargas family—your East Bay feast kept me steady.

Shout-out to Oscar Bermeo and Barbara Jane Reyes—for the chicken adobo, for the space to laugh.

Big up to Rich Villar—*juega*.

Big up to John Murillo, Tyehimba Jess, and Randall Horton—music, our lingua franca. Shout-out to Aracelis Girmay—for hearing the urgency. Shout-out to Tara Betts—for your book-lovin' self.

Big up to my VONA fam: Diem Jones—big brother almighty. Junot Díaz—for introducing me to the School of Holding Notes. David Mura—for AWP/Chicago nights and Jedi insights. Elmaz Abinader—breaking down the gangster. Evelina Galang—*kapatid na babae*. ZZ Packer—for hearing "Like Bread." Chris Abani—for asking *why*. Mat Johnson—for remembering. Suheir Hammad—*wa* star, break light. You all have been my humanity workshop over the last decade.

Big up to *all* my VONA students, past, present, and future: Don't get it twisted—you are the voices of our nation.

Shout-out for Vanessa, for the Loba cheers—you got this.

Big up to Glendaliz Camacho, Angelique Imani Rodriguez,

Kim Possible, Jessica Fillion, Karen Rossi, and Jani Rose—for knowing how to have your sister's back, and her boy's by extension.

Vaya to Angel "Tio Timbales" Rodriguez—*conguero* statesman. God bless you, bro.

Big up to Marie D. Brown—for love on the other side.

Shout-out to Tracy Sherrod—for being, always.

Big up to Tony Medina, Bonadife Rojas, Kevin Powell, Ras Baraka, Asha Bandele, Jessica Care More, Renaldo Davidson, M'Tkala, Ekere Tallie, and Mike Ladd—native tongue, forever.

Big up to Max Patiño—it was at Syracuse University where I decided on the title for the collection. Thanks for the invite.

Big up to Anthony Alonso—for being Bundini-esque.

Shout for Dimarys—for the moonlight walk on the cobblestone, and hipping me to one of the best jukeboxes in all of the Caribbean.

Big up to Andres "Velcro" Ramos—cuzzin from another dozen. Big up to Jose @ La Respuesta—*vaya*, No. 4.

Big up to Lisa Boricua Goddess—it better be you, eternally, at the door to Capicú heaven.

Big up to Jesus Papoleto Melendez and Joe Pietri—original school. Shout-out to Sandra Maria Esteves and Nancy Mercado—Nuyorican maestras.

Shout-out to Maria "Mariposa" Fernandez and Melissa "Melle Sol" Fernandez—*hermanas son de verdad.*

Shout-out to Cousin Pete Perdomo—for *Pachapo El Super Tumbao y Su Comparsa,* the last known recording on which our uncle played. Cousin Jeanette, Ray, Vilma, Provi, Bebe, Junito, Frances, and Barbara—one family. Titi Nancy and Titi Carmen—love.

Shout-out for Raquel—for faith, for our *morenita.*

Shout-out to Pablo Llanot—for listening, for making parties jump with plastic maracas, for being a *gran compañero* to Mami.

Shout-out to my father, William Perdomo—for sharing tales about my uncle. His wife, Milagros Perdomo, for welcoming my family. Shout-out to my brother, Omar Perdomo—who is quinto-ready in Tampa. Thanks for letting me record a brief interview with you at Dad's house—another portal. Shout-out to my sister, Ilia Perdomo—braveheart and dynamo. Shout-out to my niece and nephew, Isabel Perdomo-Vale and Aziel Perdomo—consider this an attempt at witnessing through our collective blood song. Big up to Anthony Vale, brand-new brother-in-law.

Quiero saludar a mi abuelo Pedro Perdomo, Sr.—R.I.P. This book is most definitely for you, too.

Shout-out to my in-laws: Mama, Papa, Alex, Mike, Mari, *y* Wandi—for the extended love.

Shout-out to my mother, Carmen Perdomo—who invented a cure for her arthritic knee by doing the shing-a-ling for breakfast.

Shout-out to my children: William Neruda, Carmen Altagracia, and BJ—call me when you get home.

Dirteater—I love you. Always. —Willie Pon.

Willie Perdomo is the author of *Where a Nickel Costs a Dime*, a finalist for the Poetry Society of America's Norma Farber First Book Award, and *Smoking Lovely*, winner of the PEN Beyond Margins Award. His work has appeared in *The New York Times Magazine, BOMB, Mandorla,* and *African Voices*. He is a Pushcart Prize nominee, a former recipient of the Woolrich Fellowship in Creative Writing at Columbia University, and a two-time New York Foundation for the Arts Poetry Fellow. He is an Instructor in English at Phillips Exeter Academy. His Web site is www.willieperdomo.com.

PENGUIN POETS

JOHN ASHBERY
Selected Poems
Self-Portrait in a Convex Mirror

TED BERRIGAN
The Sonnets

LAUREN BERRY
The Lifting Dress

JOE BONOMO
Installations

PHILIP BOOTH
Selves

JULIANNE BUCHSBAUM
The Apothecary's Heir

JIM CARROLL
Fear of Dreaming:
The Selected Poems
Living at the Movies
Void of Course

ALISON HAWTHORNE DEMING
Genius Loci
Rope

CARL DENNIS
Another Reason
Callings
New and Selected Poems 1974–2004
Practical Gods
Ranking the Wishes
Unknown Friends

DIANE DI PRIMA
Loba

STUART DISCHELL
Backwards Days
Dig Safe

STEPHEN DOBYNS
Velocities: New and Selected Poems, 1966–1992

EDWARD DORN
Way More West: New and Selected Poems

ROGER FANNING
The Middle Ages

ADAM FOULDS
The Broken Word

CARRIE FOUNTAIN
Burn Lake

AMY GERSTLER
Crown of Weeds: Poems
Dearest Creature
Ghost Girl
Medicine
Nerve Storm

EUGENE GLORIA
Drivers at the Short-Time Motel
Hoodlum Birds
My Favorite Warlord

DEBORA GREGER
By Herself
Desert Fathers, Uranium Daughters
God
Men, Women, and Ghosts
Western Art

TERRANCE HAYES
Hip Logic
Lighthead
Wind in a Box

NATHAN HOKS
The Narrow Circle

ROBERT HUNTER
Sentinel and Other Poems

MARY KARR
Viper Rum

WILLIAM KECKLER
Sanskrit of the Body

JACK KEROUAC
Book of Sketches
Book of Blues
Book of Haikus

JOANNA KLINK
Circadian
Raptus

JOANNE KYGER
As Ever: Selected Poems

ANN LAUTERBACH
Hum
If in Time: Selected Poems, 1975–2000
On a Stair
Or to Begin Again
Under the Sign

CORINNE LEE
PYX

PHILLIS LEVIN
May Day
Mercury

WILLIAM LOGAN
Macbeth in Venice
Madame X
Strange Flesh
The Whispering Gallery

ADRIAN MATEJKA
The Big Smoke
Mixology

MICHAEL MCCLURE
Huge Dreams: San Francisco and Beat Poems

DAVID MELTZER
David's Copy: The Selected Poems of David Meltzer

ROBERT MORGAN
Terroir

CAROL MUSKE-DUKES
An Octave Above Thunder
Red Trousseau
Twin Cities

ALICE NOTLEY
Culture of One
The Descent of Alette
Disobedience
In the Pines
Mysteries of Small Houses

WILLIE PERDOMO
The Essential Hits of Shorty Bon Bon

LAWRENCE RAAB
The History of Forgetting
Visible Signs: New and Selected Poems

BARBARA RAS
The Last Skin
One Hidden Stuff

MICHAEL ROBBINS
Alien vs. Predator

PATTIANN ROGERS
Generations
Holy Heathen Rhapsody
Wayfare

WILLIAM STOBB
Absentia
Nervous Systems

TRYFON TOLIDES
An Almost Pure Empty Walking

ANNE WALDMAN
Gossamurmur
Kill or Cure
Manatee/Humanity
Structure of the World Compared to a Bubble

JAMES WELCH
Riding the Earthboy 40

PHILIP WHALEN
Overtime: Selected Poems

ROBERT WRIGLEY
Anatomy of Melancholy and Other Poems
Beautiful Country
Earthly Meditations: New and Selected Poems
Lives of the Animals
Reign of Snakes

MARK YAKICH
The Importance of Peeling Potatoes in Ukraine
Unrelated Individuals Forming a Group Waiting to Cross

JOHN YAU
Borrowed Love Poems
Paradiso Diaspora